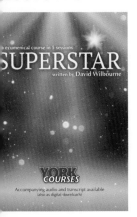

an ecumenical course in 5 sessions

SUPERSTAR

written by David Wilbourne

YORK COURSES

Accompanying audio and transcript available
(also as digital downloads)

esus Christ,
uperstar, do you
nink you're what
ney say you are?'

(Pilate to Jesus
Jesus Christ Superstar)

Before each meeting:
We suggest you read the
main text first, and then
come back to the margin
boxes. Perhaps mark a
couple of the quotations
you might like to discuss.

> What about Jesus
> Christ? I say that he was
> a precursor of idealists;
> a precursor of socialists.
> *Mikhail Gorbachev*

WHO IS JESUS

Please read: John 8.1-1

C000176036

'I dreamt I met a Gal
A most amazing mar
He had that look you
the haunting, huntea

So trills Pontius Pilate in *Jesus Christ, Superstar*. Tim Rice, who wrote the lyrics, has moved things around a bit, because in Matthew's Gospel it's Pilate's wife, not Pilate himself, who has the disturbing dream. So disturbing, that she's driven to interrupt her husband whilst his court is in session, urging him to have nothing to do with this righteous prophet who is about to cross his path [Matthew 27.19]. Perhaps she has had a chill glimpse of the future, haunted by thousands of millions chanting the creed, mentioning her husband's name and leaving him with the blame.

Of course, in a sense we all meet Christ in dreams which bridge two thousand years. Dreams, fuelled by gospel pictures so very familiar that we might wonder whether Jesus can still surprise us.

A tricky passage

The passage from John's Gospel at the head of this session (John 8.1-11) comes as a bit of a surprise, because most ancient versions of John's Gospel omit it entirely.

It begins with location, location, location. Jesus lodging at the Mount of Olives and then appearing early in the Temple at the heart of Jerusalem, the crowds forgoing their breakfast and thronging to hear him. This to-ing and fro-ing between the Mount of Olives and Jerusalem suggests a festival time, when Jerusalem was too full to contain all the pilgrims, who had to lodge outside the city walls. Maybe even Holy Week, when Jesus parked his donkey at Bethany and rode into Jerusalem.

Jesus and his adoring hearers aren't the only ones to make an early start. The Scribes and the Pharisees have been out all night, hunting like a pack, and have found their prey: an adulteress, whom they drag from her bedraggled bed. Red-faced either from shame or exertion, scantily clad, as dawn breaks she is made

> I never saw a contradiction between the ideas that sustain me and the ideas of that symbol, of that extraordinary figure, Jesus Christ.
>
> *Fidel Castro*

> What value is there in faith without works? And what are they worth if they are not united to the merits of Jesus Christ, our only good?
>
> *Saint Teresa of Avila*

> What I have come to be sure of is that what we think about the Bible's perspective on women matters, whether we consciously think about it or not... How the Bible is interpreted in relation to a woman's place before God, in the Church, in society, and in the family, matters for so many spheres of life.
>
> *Dr Lucy Peppiatt*
> *Principal of Westminster Theological Centre*

to stand and shiver in the Temple's midst and face he accusers. It's a bit of a set-up really, akin to the 'Shoul we pay taxes to Caesar or not?' scenario in Matthev 22.15-22. It's a no-win situation. If Jesus says, 'Ston her,' then, okay, he's honouring the law of Moses - bu usurping the power of Rome which, in John's Gospel scheme of things, is the only authority around that ca carry out a capital charge. If Jesus says, 'Release hei then he's turning his back on the all-important Tora - the Law that God gifted to his people on Sinai - an so they'd nail him for blasphemy.

God on trial

This is a picture of Jesus, God incarnate, on trial. familiar picture - we're always putting God on tria damning him for the defects in his creation. Thi event does have a Holy Week feel about it, wit misogyny providing a convenient excuse for a head on confrontation. And if you wanted misogyny, the the Temple was the place to go. Numbers Chapte 5 stipulates that if a husband, burning with jealousy nursed the merest suspicion that his wife was bein unfaithful, he should drag her into the temple wher she would be made to eat the dust from the floor dust poisoned by the fetid remains of animal sacrifice a veritable abattoir whose floor hadn't been moppe for decades. If somehow she survived eating th toxic dust, she was proved innocent. If she writhe in agony, miscarrying any baby she had conceivec then her guilt was proved. Jesus' reaction seems bit strange. He would have been sitting up straigh doing his teaching – even the Son of Man needs t practise class control. But when faced by the woma and her spitting accusers, he doubles up: the Gree is very emphatic at this point, κατω κυψας (*kat kupsas*) meaning 'writhing in agony'. And down a ground level, he doodles in the dust, the same toxi dust that had seen off countless innocent women.

That's a picture of Jesus that perhaps is surprising an certainly worth staying with. The same manuscript that have retained this story have a puzzling readin at the beginning of Mark's Gospel, where Jesu is confronted by a leper. Most versions reac σπλαγχνισθεις (*splangnistheis*) that he was 'movec with pity'. Our version reads: 'οργισθεις (*orgisthei* that 'he was angry'. Angry with the leper or with th leprosy? Angry that creation could turn so very nasty? Angry that community could be so fractured? God has made us to touch each other, and we utterly pervert that whenever we declare brothers and sister in Christ untouchable. We've got a similar reaction here: Jesus almost writhing in anger.

Picturing Jesus

When we picture Jesus, how do we picture him? Smiling at us, mouthing, 'Well done, good and faithful servant?' Or should we picture him writhing in agony, at us or at our plight? What makes Jesus writhe in agony in our reading? Is it the adulteress or her accusers? Well, 'No Adultery' is one of the Ten Commandments - a very serious commandment. We all too often cast God in the mode of Sergeant Wilson from *Dad's Army*: 'Oh, I'd rather you didn't commit adultery, if you don't mind, old chap!' That's not the sense of the Hebrew. The word it uses for: 'No, no Adultery', is 'LO', and has the same sense of 'No' as a mother would use shouting at her child running headlong towards the edge of a cliff: 'NOOOO!'

Just don't go there, God screams, writhing in agony to show how deadly serious he is. For God's sake, Noooo betraying one another.

But it doesn't really square with my picture of Jesus who has a track record of getting most angry, not with the sinners but with the hypocrites, who paint themselves whiter than white; who have a habit of strangling themselves by grabbing other people's throats. Hypocrisy really does make him writhe, and maybe our Lenten resolution should be to eradicate it in our own lives - banish it like smallpox.

But stay with the picture: him writhing there, doodling in the ground. What on earth was he writing? Was he just seething, turning over the dust that had killed countless women, faced by another woman who was as good as dead?

Another girl

I think he was writing: 'This is where I came in.' Dim memories of another girl betrothed to a man named Joseph – a girl who was found to be with child by another man. Stoning was reserved for betrothed girls who had sex with a man other than their fiancé. A wife who committed adultery faced execution by being strangled. Have we got the ultimate paradox here: Jesus thinking, 'Had they done this to Mum, I would never ever have been.' Had this law been carried out, Christ would never have come to birth and the world would never have been saved. No wonder he was writhing: God's ultimate rescue would have been snuffed out before it even began.

Writhing or not, the Scribes and the Pharisees persist with their accusations, Jeremy Paxman-like, keeping on and on and on: 'Should she or should she not be stoned?'

Jesus straightens up, and gives them an answer worthy of Solomon: 'Let the one amongst you who is free from sin throw the first stone at her.' The word 'sin' is drawn from the language of archery, and simply means missing the target, missing the mark, missing the bull's eye. 'Let the one amongst you who has never missed God's mark throw the first stone at her.' 'At her' - Jesus makes it personal.

The problem with modern day life is that we are safely removed from the theatre of action. If we were to personally watch cluster bombs being made in a factory in Britain, invested in by our banks, if we were to personally watch them blow the flesh off a child in Palestine, I'd like to think we'd draw back. I pray that we'd draw back.

I'd like to picture Jesus putting his arm around her at this moment, the adulteress: 'Let the one among you who is without sin throw the first stone at her and at me as well.'

But however much I might like him to have done that, it doesn't happen in this narrative. We have to wait for Good Friday for him to take all the blows and the spikes and the scorn instead of us.

Jesus stoops down again, not doubling up this time, just to return to his doodling in the toxic dust. Having pronounced the death sentence not on the woman but on the lynch mob (or rather the stone mob!) there is nothing more to be said.

They all go away, one by one, the seniors first, who have the wisdom to realise they are fallible and flawed. Only the woman remains, shivering in the dawn.

'Has no one condemned you?'
'No one, Lord.'
'Neither do I condemn you. Go, and don't sin anymore.'
My daughter, I return your life to you. Don't miss the mark anymore.

Christ the merciful

Archbishop Rowan Williams once said that folk came to God aware of how they had fallen short, trembling, approaching the terrible throne of judgement - and found it none other than a mercy seat. Rowan Williams also said that, of all the gospel stories, this story of the woman taken in adultery had the weakest manuscript evidence, but the strongest picture of Christ.

I used to have a picture of Christ in my church in Helmsley. It was actually a picture of Veronica's handkerchief, catching the legend that when Veronica wiped Christ's brow on his way to the cross, she then found her handkerchief contained a perfect image of his bloodied face. Visitors to Helmsley flocked to see it, because Christ's Calvary face was painted in such a way that the eyes could appear to be open or closed. It was trick art, an optical illusion, but if you looked at the picture, the eyes could seem to open or close before you. I had people knocking on my door claiming a miracle, offering to buy the picture, or suggesting that I whiled away my time walled-in behind the picture, moving the eyes of the Blinking Christ of Helmsley.

I found the picture spooky. I used to explain to visiting children that it was just a trick, but nevertheless, it was a picture with two messages. With his eyes closed, Christ was saying: 'I just can't bear to look,' either at naughty us, or at the terrible situation in which we find ourselves - in a sense, writhing in agony at our condition, as he writhed in agony on the temple floor. With his eyes open, Christ was saying: 'I love you so much I just can't take my eyes off you.'

But for all his shyness Jesus eventually looks the woman taken in adultery in the eyes and effectively says,
'I love you so very much,
I have given you your life back.
Off you go!'

QUESTIONS FOR GROUPS

Suggested Bible Reading: John 8.1-11

Some groups will address all the questions. That's fine. Others prefer to select just a few and spend longer on each. That's fine, too. Horses for (York) Courses!

1. According to David Wilbourne, *Jesus Christ Superstar* empowered people to dare to have a song in their soul and in their faith once again. Have you ever seen *Jesus Christ Superstar*? Do you think it is right or wrong to make a contemporary musical out of the ministry and death of Jesus?

2. **Track 2 of the audio/transcript:** Jesus was breaking the rules and infuriating the religious authorities. Is it reasonable to say Jesus was an early feminist?

3. **Track 3 of the audio/transcript:** What do you think would make Jesus writhe in anger in (a) today's world (b) today's Church?

4. **Track 4:** According to Pope Francis, 'There is simply no excuse for the church to stay shut up inside itself'. How can the church open its doors for the message to get out and the people to come in?

5. **Track 4:** What active steps do, or should, Christians take to stop terrible things from happening - either locally or globally? Or should we be content with spreading the Gospel?

6. **Track 5:** Have you ever found yourself required to, or wanting to, stand up for someone who was being bullied or unfairly accused. If so, was it a difficult - or even dangerous - decision to make?

7. Do we as Christians have an obligation to protest - be proactive - wherever we see injustice?

8. **Revisit p. 3** where David Wilbourne writes about hypocrisy. Christians are sometimes accused of having double standards - expecting God to be merciful to us but judgemental of others? Is this allegation ever justified/fair, in your opinion?

9. Should the misogynistic bits of the Bible (e.g Numbers 5; most of Leviticus) carry a health warning?

10. 'Let the one amongst you who is free from sin throw the first stone at her,' says Jesus to the crowd wanting the blood of the woman taken in adultery. Would this be a good addition to the law of our land for any conviction?

11. Jesus looked up and said to her, 'Woman, where are they? Has no one condemned you?' She said, 'No one, Lord.' And Jesus said, 'Neither do I condemn you; go, and do not sin again.' Do you think this was fair?

12. The writer Nora Ephron asserted, 'Above all, be the heroine of your life, not the victim.' How do you think Jesus would have seen himself? How do you see yourself?

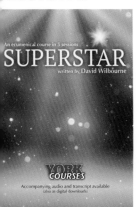

An ecumenical course in 5 sessions

SUPERSTAR

written by David Wilbourne

YORK
COURSES
Accompanying audio and transcript available
(also as digital downloads)

'Prove to me that you're divine, change my water into wine!'

(Herod to Jesus in Jesus Christ Superstar)

Coincidences are God's way of remaining anonymous.

Doris Lessing, novelist

I don't have a problem with the concept that miracles might occasionally occur at moments of great significance, where there is a message being transmitted to us by God Almighty. But as a scientist, I set my standards for miracles very high.

Francis Collins, geneticist

MIRACLES

Easter forms my core belief that not even death can put a stop to God - that every single thing is resurrectable. Given the Resurrection, surely all other miracles are possible? As the writer Saki quipped, 'When once you have taken the impossible into your calculations, its possibilities become practically limitless.'

Baby miracle

Late November 1963, when my dad was Chaplain of Hull Maternity Hospital, he was called out to baptise a baby girl, who had been born two months too soon and wasn't expected to survive. My dad held the tiny 2-pound baby for her christening, with her mum, the sister and matron looking on, a kidney dish brimful with water standing in as a font. But as he poured the water over the tiny little face, a tiny little tongue came out and licked the drops. Eagle-eyed matron noticed. 'That child's not going to die, she's a survivor. Sister, ring the consultant and tell him to come in!" she thundered. A year later to the day, a bonny toddler visited our vicarage with her grateful parents. She had survived - my dad's baptism had worked a miracle!

Sometimes miracles aren't so simple. *The Miracle of Peckham*, (from the *Only Fools and Horses* TV series) starts with Del Boy going to confession at his local church, seeking forgiveness for receiving stolen goods. The parish priest happens to mention the local hospice is facing closure. But whilst in church, Del and the priest witness a miracle: a statue of the Blessed Virgin Mary appears to be weeping.

Within days, the world's media descends on Peckham to cover the story. Del raises massive sums of money by predicting when the statue will weep again, more than enough to save the local hospice. Realising that the miracles only happen when it is raining, the parish priest finds the lead flashing on the roof above the statue is missing. Only then does it emerge that this lead was the very stolen goods Del had come to confess about! Again, we have a massive righting-of-a-wrong motif here, but with remedy and fault inextricably entwined!

Two themes

There are two themes that lie behind believing in miracles. The first is that if God can spring a mangled crucified body from a tomb, then any miracle is possible. And the second theme is where Jesus, through his miracles, is the agent of redemption seeking to right a wrong. But at the same time bearing some responsibility for the original fault - as if the Lone Ranger rides into town to sort out the mess, suddenly realising he himself made the mess in the first place.

I mentioned in the previous session how, in one ancient version of Mark 1.40, Jesus is initially angry when confronted by a leper who craves healing. It's almost as if Christ were outraged that this wasn't what Creation intended, that somehow a plethora of wrong turnings had ruined things.

Leprosy flagged up a fractured community, with no-go-zones and untouchables and the whole industry of who was clean and who was not clean. Those who are cast out by convention and social and religious order are cast in by Christ. Healing the leper is the miracle that bucks the trend, righting all the wrong turnings made by humankind, righting all the injustices perpetuated by society - jump-started by Christ's anger.

In Jesus' day, 'leprosy' was a catch-all term for all skin diseases, including eczema and anything stress-related. We realise now that stress can cause or exacerbate many illnesses, and that alleviating the stress, simply through giving the patient attention and affirmation, can have hugely beneficial results. Having Jesus, God Incarnate, accept and embrace you surely is the ultimate affirmation!

Creation's woof and warp?

But you can't explain every disease away as stress-related. Nor can you explain Christ's anger away as just a revulsion to society's revulsion to the ugly and unlovely. The blame for much disease and death, the earthquake, the tsunami, the volcanic eruption and the meteor strike cannot be laid at humankind's door, but rather seem to be Creation's very woof and warp.

Traditional Christianity has encouraged its adherents to bear such injustices with fortitude, trusting they are all part of God's plan, which will be made plain to us in the life to come. 'Here we see through a glass darkly, then we will see face to face.' (1 Corinthians 13.12).

But I don't think the miracles fit into the category of encouraging fortitude, putting up with the status quo; rather, they radically over-turn it, reversing the injustices now. Christ's anger and subsequent miracle could be daringly seen as the manufacturer's apology for the high price that has to be paid for his product to function. Mine was the fault: mine must be the cure! Is the healing of the leper and other miracles tantamount to the manufacturer's recall and refit?

In 2015 the comedian, Stephen Fry, railed against God: 'Why should I respect a capricious, mean-minded, stupid God who creates a world which is so full of injustice and pain?' Maybe Jesus' miracles are God's way of saying, 'Bear with, I'm trying to fix it!' Flagging up that one day, all will be fixed. In that light the Crucifixion can be seen as God literally holding up his hands and taking the rap, 'taking upon himself,' as the writer Alan Paton concluded: 'all the angry things, the scourge, the thorn, the nail, the utter separation.'

Some miraculous examples

The Gospels teem with miracles, and my two categories of 'echoing resurrection' and 'righting a wrong' are good starting points to try and unpack the bewildering things that are going on.

Take for example:

1. The feeding of the 5000 (Matthew 14.13-21)

2. The 180 gallons of water turned into wine at the Cana wedding (John 2.1-11)

3. The miraculous catch of fish where the trawlermen had previously toiled all night and caught nothing (Luke 5.1-11)

Before each of these three Miracles there was a situation of deadness and despair; after these Miracles there was Resurrection, life in all its fullness, nets and baskets and stone jars brim-full of it. Or to put it another way: before these Miracles, creation was taking a wrong turning, with starvation, thirst and endless toil with no reward; after the Miracle everyone is sated.

Or to take another example: the double miracle of the stilling of the storm on Lake Galilee (Mark 4.34-41) Miracle One stars someone who sleeps in the midst o the storm, has the nerve not to thrash about making things worse, but rather to simply do nothing, to be calm throughout. That is a miracle, the sure touch o one who knows that even the most chaotic storm i resurrectable. And Miracle Two, actually stilling the storm, is maybe the Creator saying, 'I so wished i could be different,' flagging up a kingdom where there will be no more dread seas.

Really wanting to be healed?

All the healing miracles fall into the obvious categor of mini-resurrections and restorations, mediated b the Easter Christ. But there is one healing miracle i John's Gospel 5.1-8 about the pool of Bethesda - the Lourdes of Palestine - where some guy has been o his stretcher for 38 years, but has never quite made i into the healing waters. Talk about NHS waiting lists Jesus asks him, 'Do you really want to be healed? which is one of the best questions in the gospel More often than not, I wonder whether we reall want things fixing, or whether we prefer things to remain the same: to play the nobody-loves-me nobody-wants-to-make-me-better game, rather than to be loved, to be made better. We prefer our warm familiar, status-quo cocoon rather than breaking ou into the cold unknown, oblivious that one day ou cocoon will become our tomb. Or, maybe, we've los our nerve - done a deal with the world and arguec miracles out of existence in order to make our faith credible.

Sometimes in my own ministry I feel bogus to the core, particularly when I visit a bereaved family. I, servant of the one who brought the dead back to life nevertheless do not raise up their loved one. Wha a fraud! Imagine a disciple of Alexander Fleming saying, 'Well yes, his antibiotic, *his* penicillin worked but I'm sorry, mine doesn't. But let me spend all m ministry explaining why!'

In his poem *Folktale*, R S Thomas pictures prayer as a knight on a quest to rescue a princess imprisoned high in a tower, hesitant because he's not sure whether she's even up there at all. (See box at foot of page.)

Even though I so often feel bogus, I've had those movement-of-a-curtain moments that make me hold on to miracles. When David Hope became Archbishop of York in 1996, we did a grand 26-day tour of the diocese. Once we visited an ancient little village school, with colourful displays and gleaming children. Glimpsing behind a screen I saw a tiny child, ashen, flat out on a PE mat. I asked the headmistress what was going on. 'Oh, he's prone to epileptic fits. We just lie him down and let him sleep it off. He's a twin, but his twin is just fine.' As it happened, that very morning at our prayers we'd read the gospel account, where the disciples fail to heal an epileptic, and have to call on Jesus (Matthew 17.14-20). 'This sort can only be cured by prayer,' he'd concluded. So I prayed for the poor little soul with all my heart. He didn't get up though.

Years later I came across the headmistress again. 'That little boy - the twin, the epileptic - what happened to him?' I asked, as we reminisced about the Archbishop's visit. 'It's funny you should mention that,' she replied. 'David Hope must be a holy man, because that little lad never had a fit again. Several of my staff had received training on handling epilepsy, that wasn't needed!'

If only we could recover our nerve and expect miracles. Be the miracle. Do you want to be healed? Dare you let resurrection in?

'He brought light out of darkness,
not out of a lesser light.
He can bring thy summer out of winter
though thou have no spring.'

John Donne

'I would
have refrained long since,'
the knight admits,
'but that peering once
through my locked fingers
I thought I detected
the movement of a curtain.'
From R S Thomas' poem *Folktale*

QUESTIONS FOR GROUPS

Suggested Bible Reading: Matthew 19.26

1. What is your definition of a miracle?

2. Do you believe in miracles? Has a miracle you personally desired and prayed for actually happened?

3. **Track 8 of the audio/transcript:** 'Easter forms my core belief that not even death can put a stop to God - that every single thing is resurrectable.' Are some things too broke to fix?

4. **Track 9 of the audio/transcript:** 'Or, maybe, we've lost our nerve - done a deal with the world and argued miracles out of existence in order to make our faith credible.' Do you agree? Is having to believe in miracles a challenge to your faith?

5. **Track 10:** Why does God break into some situations, but seems absent in others?

6. **Track 11:** What experience have you had of R S Thomas' 'movement of a curtain'? What glimpses sustain your faith/belief?

7. Jesus often said to the healed person, 'Your faith has cured you.' Can you have a miracle without faith?

8. **Revisit *The Miracle of Peckham* anecdote on p.7.** Does it matter if you do the right thing for the wrong reasons?

9. **Revisit *Two Themes* on p.8.** 'There are two themes that lie behind believing in miracles.' Are you convinced by either of them?

10. **On p.9** David asks: 'Is the healing of the leper and other miracles tantamount to the manufacturer's recall and refit?' What do you think?

11. **Re-visit *Really wanting to be healed?* on p.10.** Do you agree with the old adage: 'God helps those who help themselves'?

12. Are miracles about how you view the world? If you look for the positive in things, do you find it?

13. **On p.10** David writes: 'More often than not, I wonder whether we really want things fixing, or whether we prefer things to remain the same.' Is this true? If so, why don't we want things fixing?

THE PSALMS

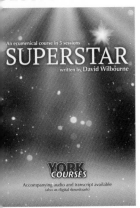

Jesus Christ Superstar's lengthy ballad in the garden of Gethsemane catches the spirit of Jesus well here. In fact, it catches the spirit of every Orthodox Jew, with 150 ballads to choose from, which ran the gamut of life and death, hope and despair, celebrating a God as close as touch, yet simultaneously a God so far away you wondered if he existed at all. Those 150 ballads we know as the Psalms.

Here are ten reasons why the Psalms should fire our spirit too:

1. The Psalms were written in Hebrew

Hebrew letters and back-to-front words are strange to us, with the reader even having to supply the missing vowels. *Prs y th Lrd* is all you'd have had for the first line of a well-known hymn. You would have had to engage with the text, supply the vowels, deciding that *Praise ye the Lord* had the edge on *Press ye the Lard!* Or you would have learned the vowels - and therefore the Psalms - off by heart, again engaging with them as they soaked into your very soul.

Even though we have vowels in English, the Hebrew principle is still there - we say the same Psalms daily, week by week, so that they sink down deep. A public school boy was fed up with chanting psalm after psalm at compulsory Morning and Evening Prayer. But when as a soldier he suffered the deprivations of a Japanese POW camp, he was grateful that the Psalms were there, deep down, keeping him faithful in the midst of awful brutality. Psalms are worth learning off by heart, just as some hymns are worth learning off by heart, because they provide words for our inarticulate faith.

2. The Psalms are poems that don't rhyme

'Not poems then!' you might think. Except that Hebrew rules for poetry are different from English rules. Rather than rhyming they repeat themselves, cleverly using different words, running through a

'I only want to say, if there is a way, take this cup away from me, I don't want to taste its poison...'

(Jesus to his Father in *Jesus Christ Superstar*)

The Psalms are a reality check to keep prayer from becoming sentimental, superficial, or detached from the real world.
Richard H Schmidt, priest

The psalms provide wisdom for navigating our way through the challenges and delights of life.
Bishop Stephen Cottrell in York Course The Psalms

veritable thesaurus to hammer home the point. It's called parallelism:

Set a guard O Lord on my lips:
and keep the door of my mouth.

I will not allow my eyes to sleep:
nor let my eyelids slumber.

It's repetition yet it isn't repetition. Using parallelism and couplets - two lines that seem to say the same thing - is a clever way of letting teaching sink in. Anglicans have five of the Psalm couplets in the versicles and responses at Evensong such as:

O God make speed to save us:
O Lord make haste to help us.

Because there's so much of this parallelism around, many churches break up every verse of every Psalm in English into two, and stick a colon between them. And the custom is to make a short pause at that colon, take a breath in the middle of the verse.

3. The Psalms are busy

All 150 of them catch the whole of life. When Psalms are used in worship they often stop, with a colon, in the middle of each verse - as we should stop in the middle of our hectic Psalm-like lives. Their pauses only amplify their eloquence, like the pause in Handel's *Hallelujah Chorus* before the final *Hallelujah*. By our pauses we'll be judged.

4. The Psalms are 'warts-and-all' with no punches pulled

The depths are there as well as the heights, the despair and the joy, the sweet and the sour, of faith and of life.

My God, my God, why have you forsaken me?
(Psalm 22.1)

My soul waits for the Lord:
more than the night-watch for the morning.
(Psalm 130.6)

Behold how good and joyful a thing it is:
when brothers dwell together in unity.
(Psalm 133.1)

Blessed shall he be that taketh thy children:
and throweth them against the stones.
(Psalm 137.9)

The whole of human existence is there, both that which makes us immensely proud and immensely ashamed. The Psalms are a mirror of selves, not the selves we pretend to be, not the facades we like to project, but our true, marvellous, awful selves, nevertheless loved by God. The Psalms trumpet our darkest viciousness and yet God still loves us.

The Psalms allow us to lament before God about our current ills, permitting us to also lament elsewhere. A faith that claims it is improper to lament before God depicts a false God, who only wants our praise and adulation. This soon spills over into a life where one is not allowed to lament, not allowed to question and rail against the status quo, within schools, hospitals, government or the courts. The order of the day becomes absolute, beyond question, and we are left only with grim obedience and voiceless despair. The Psalms point us in another direction: as Dylan Thomas put it, 'to rage, rage against the dying of the light' and find health and wholeness therein.

5. The Psalms are communal

They are not so much personal or individual, but are rather communal (like the National Anthem) made to be sung together, a faith anthem, anthems of Judaism and Christianity through the ages. Sometimes there'll be bits of the Psalms that say nothing to our condition. But they will speak to others, for others, and, in effect, when we say them, we stand with those others. Maybe we don't feel like throwing children against stones, maybe we never have. But someone in our world is feeling like that, doing that. And when we say that verse from Psalm 137 we enter into their mindset and shiver and say, 'There but for the grace of God...' And in some mysterious sense there is an inkling of redemption, both for us and for the monsters and their victims.

6. The Psalms are also personal

Whilst they are communal, the Psalms are also personal, with an ease of movement between the plural and the singular, between the individual and the community. Many of the Psalms originate with a person: David, Israel's legendary king, who loved fiercely, fought fiercely, wheeled and dealed fiercely, and played the harp fiercely to soothe the savage breast.

The Old Testament spends more words on David than it does on anyone else - only Jesus, (titled 'the son of David') gets more words, when it comes to the New Testament. This massive breadth of exciting experience, the highest and the lowest points of human existence, are channelled into David's Psalms. He was the Leonard Cohen of his age!

Of course David didn't write them all - David never sat and wept by the waters of Babylon. But he set the style; he started the hymn book which then gathered other similar hymns as time went on; a liturgical snowball, growing as it rolls down the hills of time.

7. The Psalms are incarnational

As well as being rooted in one definite life, the Psalms are incarnational - rooted in all life. Sailors, farmers, dragons, whales, storms, snow, dancing girls and cymbals are all there, celebrated as being a valued part of God's massive span - a God for whom there is absolutely no limit. No one who sings the Psalms can set a boundary to God's scope.

8. The Psalms are great prose poetry

That breadth of God's activity is caught through some of the most marvellous prose poetry ever written, whatever the translation. For instance:

I will lift up mine eyes to the hills:
from whence cometh my help.
(Psalm 121.1)

9. The Psalms have deep insight into God's nature and purpose

Closely allied to this prose poetry are the Psalms' deep insights into God that arrest you, stopping you short in your tracks.

For with thee is the well of life:
and in thy light shall we see light.
(Psalm 36.9)

The ultimate is the last verse of Psalm 17 that catches the destiny of us all:
When I awake and see you as you are:
then I shall be satisfied.
(Psalm 17.15)

10. The Psalms are written to be sung by Christ

The Psalms are written to be sung by Christ, who is the undoubted destiny of us all. *Jesus Christ Superstar* commends Christ's story not as a flat narrative, but as a musical. Luke's Gospel, if you think about it, is a musical, with its *Benedictuses* and *Magnificats* and *Glorias* and *Nunc Dimittises*. Every gospel deserves to be sung with joy in your heart rather than said in a dull monotone. *Jesus Christ Superstar* empowered people to dare to have a song in their soul and in their faith once again.

The Psalms are written to be sung by Christ, and only as Christ can we sing them. Who are we, with our imperfections, to rail at God? Who are we, with all the motes in our eyes, to voice where others fall short so eloquently? Who are we to protest at our innocence? How can we flatter ourselves that Almighty God would be pleased with our puny praise? Who are we to map God's span?

Only Christ, as history's one and only perfect man, has the right to sing the words. Only Christ has the theological range to span the Psalms' octaves. Only Christ, history's total innocent, can call for his enemies to be broken.

And yet he never did. From Psalm 3.7 he takes *'Break the teeth of the ungodly, O Lord'* and transforms it into 'Father, forgive them.' As St Augustine declared, Christ makes his own the attitude of even his enemies and transforms it. He found a way!

QUESTIONS FOR GROUPS

Suggested Bible Reading: Psalm 27.1

1. In his closing reflection Stephen Wigley recalls a musical highlight from his life. Is there a piece of music that has made a profound impact on you?

2. **Track 13 of the audio/transcript:** David Wilbourne writes, '150 ballads to choose from, which ran the gamut of life and death, hope and despair, celebrating a God as close as touch, yet simultaneously a God so far away you wondered if he existed at all.' Is God close enough for you to touch him - or so far away as to be virtually non-existent?

3. **On Track 13 of the audio/transcript** Steve Chalke tells of Mother Teresa's experience of God. Do you find her story surprising/shocking/encouraging...?

4. **On p. 14** David claims, 'The Psalms are warts-and-all with no punches pulled'. And on **track 14** the participants discuss the ending of Psalm 137.9: *'Happy shall they be who take your little ones and dash them against the rock!'* Where is God's grace for those monsters who do throw children against rocks?

5. **Track 14:** What do you think of the advice that Bishop Anthony Bloom gave to Carmody Grey's mother? What solution might you have offered – or have wanted to hear?

6. David claims that the Book of Psalms catches 'the whole of life'. Does this still hold true today? For instance, have the Psalms got anything to say about work-life balance, equality for women, or sex, even? Our participants discuss this on **track 15**.

7. David writes: 'Psalms are worth learning off by heart, because they provide words for our inarticulate faith.' Do you find the Psalms helpful in expressing your faith?

8. **Revisit track 16 and point 3 on p. 14:** 'By our pauses we'll be judged.' Is it fair that we are judged by the use we make of the pauses in our busy lives? In other words, how do you spend your downtime?

9. There is a lot of 'railing against' and 'lamenting over' in the Psalms. Most of us have railed and lamented at times over different things. But what can we do to change things?

10. **Track 16:** Carmody Grey says, 'We're going to be judged on the whole of our life, not on the religious bits of it.' Do you think God is going to judge us at all? And if so, how and when?

11. 'It's the thought that counts' according to the adage. Is it - or is it the deed?

12. Read the words of Richard H Schmidt in the box on p. 13. Do you agree that the Psalms are a reality check?

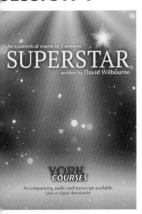

An ecumenical course in 5 sessions

SUPERSTAR
written by David Wilbourne

YORK COURSES

Accompanying audio and transcript available
(also as digital downloads)

**'I don't know
how to love him.'**

(Mary Magdalene to
Jesus in *Jesus Christ
Superstar*)

Shug say, Celie, tell the truth, have you ever found God in church? I never did. I just found a bunch of folks hoping for him to show. Any God I ever felt in church I brought in with me. And I think all the other folks did too. They come to church to share God, not find God.

Some folks didn't have him to share, I said.

From Alice Walker's novel The Color Purple

THE CHURCH

'I don't know how to love him,' Mary Magdalene confesses in *Jesus Christ Superstar*. So cool, no lover's fool, yet totally non-plussed when it comes to trying to love Christ, scared stiff by the enormity of the task.

Missing God

'I don't know how to love him' is the song of the Church throughout the ages, trying so very hard, but missing him again and again. 'Such a fast God,' claimed R S Thomas in his poem *Pilgrimages*, 'always before us and leaving as we arrive.' Every church has that atmosphere, caught so well by Nick Hornby in his novel *How to be Good,* that this may have been God's house once, but God has clearly moved, shut up shop, and gone elsewhere.

But rather than that being a downer, I think it is an excellent starting point. Because a church which claimed to have got God pat, which claimed to contain him in his entirety would actually be misrepresenting God and would contain nothing more than an idol. If the Easter God can spring out of tombs he is not to be contained by any building. 'The whole world cannot contain you,' Solomon admits at the dedication of his mighty temple, 'how much less this house that I have built.'

Seeing church as a place where we can be real and not artificially good seems an excellent preparation for a God before whom we can only be real. There's no fooling God.

Peter and the Church in denial

The account of Peter's denial in all four Gospels is real (Mark 14.66-end and parallels), stripping discipleship and vocation and faith to the bare bones. This is what is left when all the games have stopped: the cold dawn, the glare of torches, the grinning faces that might laugh it off, or lynch you themselves. This is true reality without the veneers.

Peter, gathered with the servants, warming their hands around the fire whilst Jesus shivers at the trial that awaits him, is a very powerful picture of the Church. Perhaps not the picture we prefer. We may like to fantasise about the Church being the body of Christ, our hands being Christ's hands to bless his world, our mouth being Christ's mouth to preach his words of grace, our feet being Christ's feet to run for him and his Gospel. As fantasies go, it is a marvellous one. But I really do believe that a better image is of the Church being a group of people who gather together on a cold night, warming their hands around a fire whilst their Lord is brutalised off-stage.

At first sight it is an image that is bleak and bald. And yet, it is a good image in that the two centres of action are not separate from each other, but affect and inform each other. The Lord turns and looks at Peter. Peter remembers his words. Peter goes out and weeps bitterly. That's liturgy at its very best. Every church busy, busy, busy with its activity, keeping the fire going so that hands will be warm (or warm-ish!), nevertheless, out the corner of its eye, sees its Lord brutalised off-stage, and that seeing makes a world of difference.

Of course, those who gathered around the fire on that first Maundy Thursday were a motley bunch - believers and questioners, disciples and non-disciples: in other words, a church! And their two-way conversation affects each other. Don't be too hard on Peter, because there was obviously something about him that made him stand out. He wasn't just one of the lads or lasses warming himself. The conversation could have gone another way. The servant girl saying, 'Well, one thing's for sure, Peter, you're not one of that lot.' Someone else saying, 'You're one of the lads, Peter, not one of these religious freaks.'

Before ordination I worked in Barclays Bank in Hull. When my colleagues realised where I was heading, they said that I was the last person they thought should become a vicar, I was too normal. I remember being rather proud of that image - perhaps I should have heard a cockerel crowing! If Christianity were a crime, would the authorities have enough on any of us in the church to secure a conviction? 'No, surely not, you can't be a Christian, you're just one of the lads, one of the girls...'

Instead of being just a church that welcomes and receives by keeping the doors open, let us try also to be a church that finds new roads, that is able to step outside itself and go to those who do not attend Mass, to those who have quit or are indifferent.

Pope Francis

Facing our reality

Any church worth its salt chips away at us, enabling us bit by bit to face our reality and realise that we are more, much more than one of the lads, one of the girls, in that we are called not so much to be a little lower than the angels, but to be Christ.

Any church worth its salt feeds us on Christ. Christ might not be palatable: the young man in the gospel turned away, because his riches could not stomach Christ's call (Luke 18.18-24). But nevertheless, a church should encourage us to be real and feed us on Christ's reality. The Eucharist, Holy Communion, Mass, the heartbeat of the Church, re-enacting Christ's brutalisation, is symbolic of feeding on Christ. The Church is not so much a rest-home for the weary, but a canteen for the troops - Christ's SAS. If you want an army to win, you feed them the best. 'An army marches on its stomach,' according to Napoleon. We need to feed Christ's army on Christ and his love.

Wouldn't it be simply wonderful if you spotted a wayside pulpit outside a church which said: 'For our Mission Statement, see 1 Corinthians 13.' Our mission statement when I was a parish priest in Helmsley was: 'God's so priceless he comes free.' Because love comes free, love cannot be bought, love cannot be earned, love cannot be forced. I heard about a parish in South Wales that was charging £100 a baptism. That made me angry and ashamed, both that people were being fleeced, but more so that someone had dared, like Judas, to put a price on Christ's head. And as Judas learned to his cost, Christ's head is not for pricing, because that is the very opposite of what a church should be: we should feed folk on Christ who is so priceless he comes without charge.

And Mary Magdalene in *Jesus Christ Superstar* agonised over that. Tradition has it that the girl who 'had had so many men before in very many ways' had tried to put a price on love, buying and selling love like the traders in the Temple bought and sold doves. And then along came Jesus and overturned the tables and made Mary realise that the sort of love he embodied could not be bought or sold. Maybe that's a cue for another wayside pulpit. 'This Church has ceased trading because love comes free.'

La's orchestra, in *La's orchestra saves the world* by Alexander McCall Smith, though a lowly amateur thing based in a tiny Suffolk village, actually outplays the massive cosmic events that are going on around it: the Second World war, the Cold War, the threat of nuclear annihilation. La quietly encouraged all the amateur musicians she gathered around her to play as beautifully as they could, to move and soothe a troubled world. This would present an antithesis to the anger and fear that could unleash missiles, and through music show the face of love, and forgiveness. The Church is called to be a boy David quietening the troubled King Sauls of the world with its sweet harp-playing.

All aboard

But probably the main image for the Church is to see it as a boat, which is why the centre of any church building is called the nave - Latin for 'ship'. But what sort of ship? Is the ship in dock, rusting, with the crew stirring itself to apply a lick of paint every now and again? Is the ship a cruise liner, with passengers expecting constant entertainment from the captain and his crew? Is the ship a cargo vessel carrying precious commodities to feed a hungry world? Or is the ship a lifeboat? All hands on deck - no leisurely time to discuss whether the crew should be women or men, traditional, catholic or charismatic, or what sexual orientation or practice is permissible when lifeboat's the name and saving lives at sea's the game. Or is the ship an ark with Reverend Captain Noah scratching his head at all the strange pairs of creatures who take refuge therein? Or is the Church like SS *Enterprise* in *Star Trek*, boldly going where no man has gone before or, hesitatingly, going where God has gone before?

Whatever they are called to be, or fail to be called to be, churches are, in Philip Larkin's marvellous phrase, 'serious places on serious earth.'

We don't know how to love Him, but at least we try!

Read John 12.20-36 before the final session - or make sure you have a Bible handy!

QUESTIONS FOR GROUPS

Suggested Bible Reading: 1 Peter 2.9-10

1. **Track 18 of the audio/transcript:** Looking at your church as an orchestra, which instrument do you play? Who's the conductor? Is there room for more than one conductor?

2. **Track 19 of the audio/transcript.** On p. 21 David writes: 'Any Church worth its salt feeds us on Christ. Christ might not be palatable.' What are the unpalatable things that you might have difficulty teaching?

3. **Track 19:** In answering the question: 'What are the unpalatable things that you might have difficulty teaching?' Catherine Fox chooses the 'scandal of particularity'. Do you sympathise with her difficulty?

4. **Track 20:** In the old days the church was full of people who went to church because it was expected/the thing to do. Is it better to have today's emptier churches - with fewer church-goers who really want to be there? Do you agree with Carmody Grey's views on this?

5. **On pp. 19 & 20** David writes that Peter and the servants warming their hands around a fire, whilst their Lord is brutalised off-stage, is a very powerful picture of the Church. What brutalities do you think that the Church is failing to see today?

6. 'Such a fast God,' claimed the poet R S Thomas in his poem *Pilgrimages*, 'always before us and leaving as we arrive.' Can you identify with this image of God? In which place(s) do you feel God's presence most strongly?

7. What does your local church do that makes you feel real/alive/engaged/ enthusiastic...?

8. **Track 22:** Stephen Wigley suggests that the soul song *People get ready, there's a train coming* 'raises for us the challenging question about whether the Church we know now is the empty building which God has left – or the journey into God's future that we're invited to make in the company of Jesus?' Perhaps it's both? Is the church, in its often near-empty state, no longer the place where God is to be found?

9. **On p. 21** David Wilbourne asserts: 'The Church is not so much a rest-home for the weary, but a canteen for the troops - Christ's SAS.' Discuss!

10. **On p. 22** David uses the well-known analogy of the Church as a ship (an ark, a lifeboat, a cargo vessel, a cruise liner - even a spaceship). Will a local church need to reinvent itself from time to time?

11. When - if ever - is it acceptable for a church or cathedral to ask for money from people who visit? (E.g. concert; baptism; wedding; sight-seeing...)

12. **Revisit Catherine Fox's words on track 21.** Should the Church be leading in the issue of global warming?[1]

[1]An entire (and startling) course *Caring for Creation* is in preparation for Lent 2021. Watch this space!

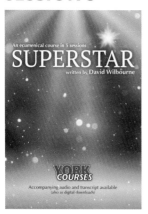

An ecumenical course in 5 sessions

SUPERSTAR
written by David Wilbourne

YORK COURSES

Accompanying audio and transcript available
(also as digital downloads)

'Did you mean to die like that, was that a mistake or did you know your messy death would be a record-breaker?'

(Judas to Jesus in *Jesus Christ Superstar*)

> The trajectory of all human life is to die – and dying, whenever it happens, is not a failure or a mistake, on our part or God's. Yes, for some of us, death comes earlier, more tragically, or more painfully than for others, *but it's still what's supposed to happen in the end.*
>
> *Revd Wendy Bray*
>
> If it has to choose who is to be crucified, the crowd will always save Barabbas.
>
> *Jean Cocteau, writer*

CROSS PURPOSES

We like to pretend we understand our every action and emotion. But if we're honest, we admit that we haven't got much of a clue about why we are as we are, why we do what we do, and how we react when stuff happens. Most of the time we are trying our best in the midst of an utter storm; we are all at sea. Life is the ultimate Sudoku[1] or crossword which we puzzle over and over, but never manage to work out. Or if we do get it out, it's invariably wrong.

And in the midst of a Sudoku of a life, there is nothing more puzzling and mysterious than suffering and pain - our own and that of others, where we may play either the role of victim or persecutor. Sometimes suffering happens to us; sometimes we cause it. And that's life.

And that's life

Holy Week, the heart of the Christian faith, majors on 'why suffering?' Why did Christ suffer and die? What has his suffering and death to do with our suffering and death? This ultimate Sudoku is set out for us in the Passion narratives in the Gospels and the Epistles, as the New Testament writers try to puzzle out the cross and offer some clues.

I don't think anyone's cracked it. Some people think they have, claiming that Jesus died because of this, that he died in order to achieve that: for instance, Mrs C F Alexander's verse in the hymn *There is a green hill far away*:

> '*He died that we might be forgiven,
> he died to make us good,
> that we might go at last to heaven,
> saved by his precious blood.*'

Good try, Mrs Alexander - you've put the numbers in the puzzle rather than leave it empty, but they don't quite fit; they don't quite add up.

I believe that although suffering is the ultimate Sudoku, it is solvable. It's just that no one has solved it yet, like those seven Millennium Maths problems that you get a million dollars for solving![2] But through

[1]For those who haven't succumbed to Sudoku yet, it is a numbers-in-a-grid game that is in most newspapers and ranges from 'easy' to 'super-fiendish

the New Testament and through the Church, God has essentially given us his word that the suffering and death of Jesus is the key to the puzzle.

Chipping away at the wall

My approach to Sudoku is to keep on chipping away, leave it for a bit and then return, take a different tack, dare to be a bit off-the-wall to make a break through. Like John 12.20-36 is a bit off-the-wall - it would be a good idea to read the passage at this point.

So the Greeks, representing the rest of the world, make the request, 'Sir, we want to see Jesus.' But the Jesus that Jesus offers them isn't a honey-tongued Greek philosopher, or a superstar, but simply a man being 'lifted up', either to be crucified or glorified - the Greek 'υψοω (*hupsoō*) is deliberately ambiguous.

Jesus is using imagery that harks back over a thousand years to when the Israelites, having escaped from Egypt, spent 40 years in the wilderness before they finally reach Canaan, God's Promised Land. They repeatedly lost the plot and lost the faith, and at one stage they were terrified by killer snakes, which they saw as a punishment sent by God because of their faithlessness. Moses' solution was to make a bronze snake, nail it to a pole and raise it up high. Any Israelite who had been bitten by a snake, by fixing their eyes on the bronze image, miraculously was unaffected by the deadly snakebite.

As solutions go, that was quite off-the-wall. What was going on there? Maybe it was to do with looking at what harms you to heal you. We spend a lot, if not most, of our life in denial, avoiding our fears, or investing in quite complex systems to avoid real and imaginary fears. In cocooning ourselves we can often limit, or even deny, the very life and chance of life we are trying to protect. The cocoon can become our tomb. Dare to look at what harms you to heal you. The situations, the people, look them straight in the eye and be prepared to be surprised rather than exterminated.

[2] The Millennium Prize Problems are seven problems in mathematics that were stated by the Clay Mathematics Institute on May 24, 2000. US$1 million prize will be awarded by the Institute to the discoverer(s) of an answer to any of the Problems

Most snakebites are not deadly in themselves - it's your body's reaction, the adrenalin, the shock, which can kill you. Maybe the bronze snake on the stake advertised that these snakes were mortal, fallible. Rather than them defeating us, we could defeat them. We could nail them up, put them in their place.

According to John 3.14-15, Jesus said, 'As Moses lifted up the snake in the wilderness so will the Son of Man be lifted up.' (And he talks about that lifting up being his very glorification.) In the other Gospels you have him agonising in Gethsemane about the fate that awaits him, sweating drops of blood: 'I only want to say, if there is a way...' But in John we have a supremely calm and sure Jesus: 'What am I to say "Father save me from this hour"? No, it was for this that I came to this hour.' 'I have come to be lifted up like the bronze snake was lifted up in the wilderness. I suppose we are surrounded by fears - venomous fears - of pain, rejection, suffering, losing our reason, death. Deadly snakes to the left and right of us. 'Look at me, lifted up,' Jesus says, 'and that will be your cure.' 'Trust in me,' he is saying, 'I am the solution to the ultimate puzzle of suffering and death. I am the answer, lifted up on the cross.'

The answer's in the cross

So how is the cross the answer? We just need to have faith that Jesus has given us his word on that, and then in the cross see hints of a solution, then spend our lives exploring, and enjoying exploring, the hints. One path I have found very revealing and helpful is to see the cross as God nailed up, God-with-us in our darkness. *'God is weak and powerless in the world, and that is exactly the way, the only way, he can be with us and help us,'* claimed Dietrich Bonhoeffer, the German pastor and theologian who was murdered by the Nazis. He eloquently expressed the heart of the Christian Gospel of a God who is impaled on suffering, as did the Welsh priest-poet RS Thomas:

*'This Christmas before
an altar of gold
the holly will remind
us how love bleeds.'*

The Cross, God-nailed-up, challenges the idea of

some distant God who created the universe and then withdrew from the field of play, giving us an odd but distant cheer now and again. The Cross proclaims a God caught up in it all, suffering as we suffer, making it very clear that we do not suffer alone but that he, the light of lights, is beside us in our particular darkness.

Also, God being nailed up invites us to move on from the image of the omnipotent, all-powerful, all-judging, all-terrible God, fire and lightening coming out of his mouth and consuming unworthy old us. We probably all have that image of God in our subconscious: a God who is a monster and out to get us. Instead, dare we see a self-emptying God who is a victim amongst victims? Though we may approach in dread God on a throne of terrible judgement, instead we are faced by a beaten-up man bearing the terrible marks of crucifixion, sitting on none other than a mercy seat.

Throne of judgement to mercy seat

Recently I've been researching 14th century Norwich, when it was clearly far from the sleepy place we know and love today. There were unpaid mercenaries returning from the Hundred Years' War with France, looting and pillaging. The Black Death and the Plague were halving the population. There was the threat of revolution, and the peasants rising up and executing the Archbishop of Canterbury. There were religious extremists who wanted to do away with all bishops!

During all this turbulence the Church was screaming about an angry, judgemental God. Bishop Dispenser, Bishop of Norwich, rather than don robes, wore a suit of armour. He used confession as entrapment, for if there was a whiff of treason, he had the supplicant arrested, found guilty and executed. Turbulence is not a new phenomenon.

But in the midst of all this, Mother Julian of Norwich bravely declared that there was no wrath whatsoever in God. No wrath because we have spoiled his creation, nor for wilfully wrecking our lives. No wrath whatsoever. The Cross didn't slake God's wrath, it slaked ours, with a mother-like God, infinitely gentle, infinitely suffering, physically opening his heart to let his love, like a divine sea, flow into our arid stench-

> I could never myself believe in God, if it were not for the cross ... In the real world of pain, how could one worship a God who was immune from it?
>
> *Dr John Stott*

> Love. The power of love ... Love not just as a sentiment, but as a strategy. Through the ultimate sacrifice of his life – death on the cross – he transformed that cross from an instrument of the most horrendous torture to a tool for liberation – eternal freedom. Jesus Christ our Saviour.
>
> *Paul Boateng, politician*

> The crucifixion should never be depicted. It is a horror to be veiled.
>
> *William Golding*

ridden creeks and enable life, forgiveness and acceptance to flourish.

A lot of wrath in humankind, but no wrath in God. God is total love, a love that (according to 1 Corinthians 13) is patient and kind, keeping no score of wrongs. We ought to catch his habit. How about instead of no meat on Fridays, no wrath on Fridays, just for the day?

When the Plague nearly killed young Mother Julian it sparked off an intense vision of the crucifixion. In her fevered state, as Jesus bleeds and suffers terribly before her, Julian actually converses with Jesus on the Cross. She realises that the purpose of the Cross is not to satisfy God's wrath but ours. 'Are you satisfied that I love you?' Jesus asked. 'If I could suffer more I would suffer more to win your heart.' As the spear is driven into his side and water and blood gush out Julian sees the world being flooded with God's love, a tsunami of love.

See, from his head, his hands, his feet,
sorrow and love flow mingled down.
Did e'er such love and sorrow meet,
or thorns compose so rich a crown?

(Isaac Watts)

'Did you mean to die like that? Was that a mistake?' No mistake, Judas, but a divine answer to a question that is literally a matter of life and death!

Closing Prayer:

Lord Jesus Christ,
Son of the Father,
Renew my Friendship in You;
And help me to Serve You
With a Quiet Mind and a Burning Spirit